PRESCRIPTION: Financial FAST

Frances Armfield

PRESCRIPTION: Financial FAST

Frances Armfield

Frances Armfield

Prescription - Financial Fast
Frances Armfield

Copyright © Frances Armfield
Published By Parables
September, 2018

All Rights Reserved. No part of this book may be reproduced or utilized in any form or by any means, electronic or mechanical, including photocopying, recording, or by any information storage and retrieval system, without permission in writing from the author.

Unless otherwise specified Scripture quotations are taken from the authorized version of the King James Bible.

ISBN 978-1-945698-69-9
Printed in the United States of America

Readers should be aware that Internet Web sites offered as citations and/or sources for further information may have been changed or disappeared between the time this was written and when it is read.

PRESCRIPTION: Financial FAST

Frances Armfield

Frances Armfield

CONTENTS

Acknowledgements   10

Introduction   11

In the Beginning   13
1. The Notice
2. Financial Revelation
3. The Vision

Financial FAST   21
4. What is a Financial FAST?
5. Why do I need a Financial FAST?
6. How did I get here?

Leap of Faith   39
7. Necessity or Nicety?
8. Back to the Basics - FASTing
9. Continuous Action

Reflections   54

11. Breaking the FAST

Financial FAST Tables   56

Action Plan Notes   59

Scriptures   61

Prayers   63

Matthew 6: 19-21 (ESV)
"Do not lay up for yourselves treasures on earth, where moth and rust destroy and where thieves break in and steal, but lay up for yourselves treasures in heaven, where neither moth nor rust destroys and where thieves do not break in and steal. For where your treasure is, there your heart will be also."

Frances Armfield

PRESCRIPTION: Financial FAST

Beginning Prayer:

Lord, I am surrendering my earthly pursuits to honor you. As I read and complete the assessments in this book, along with studying scriptures, please assist me in being honest with myself. Also, reveal any thoughts, beliefs, and misunderstandings that I need to repent of concerning my feelings about You and myself. You have been good to me, so good that You sent Jesus, your one and only son, as a living sacrifice to save me. You have entrusted me with finances and the gifts to produce wealth, so I pray for wisdom to make the right choices daily. Empower me to honestly and faithfully use my resources for Your glory through giving, praying, and fasting.

In Jesus' name, Amen!

Ecclesiastes 7:11-13 (NLT)
Wisdom is even better when you have money. Both are a benefit as you go through life. Wisdom and money can get you almost anything, but only wisdom can save your life. Accept the way God does things, for who can straighten what He has made crooked?

Frances Armfield

ACKNOWLEDGEMENTS

All the glory goes to God because He put the message of this book in my dreams. I am truly grateful that He chose or trusted me to package and deliver His message.

I did not grow up in ministry, but I had grandmothers who instilled faith in me at an early age. They taught me to have faith in God, as well as love others without always trying to please everyone. Life was hard until I understood those lessons in my heart. Know and understand that God never gives up on us and He uses every opportunity in our lives to guide us to our destiny.

I am thank for …!

My beloved husband, God knew we needed each other! Thank you for continuously encouraging, supporting, and have patience with me through all the trials, uncertainties, and excitement of writing this book.

My adored children, I also thank you for your patience and understanding through my times of self-doubt, frustration, and happy days of writing.

The reader of this book, my prayer is that this book answers prayers as well as encourages obedience and helps you to trust God, step out on faith, and inspire others to do the same through my testimony. This book was written to be a tool to recognize the need for God in our finances and assist in unlocking in addition to seeing His promises in our lives. It is a useful tool to be used for encouragement as often as necessary so that we continue to encounter God. Enjoy!

Many Blessings,

Frances

INTRODUCTION

God's Perspective on Financial Wellness

Quick question to ponder: Are you being obedient with the resources God has provided you to advance His kingdom?

God is at work in all that happens in our lives and has placed purpose in all our experiences. He uses our everyday experiences to benefit our lives as well as others. Some ways we experience Him is through the Holy Spirit. The Holy Spirit initiates prayer and maturity in His word through:

- Conviction
- Warning and correcting
- Trust in Him
- Purity and preparation
- Benefits for others

Financial wellness reflects our good stewardship of the financial blessings God has bestowed on us.

In the Bible, Matthew wrote, "No one can serve two masters; for either you will hate the one and love the other, or you will stand by and be devoted to the one and despise and be against the other. You cannot serve both God and money" (Matthew 6:24 AMP). This verse, along with our financial status, whether wealthy, dealing with financial hardship, or somewhere in between, urges us to evaluate our relationship with God, money, and others.

Even if we are financially stable (wealthy or stable), questions arise regarding whether or not we are using our financial gifts as God intends.

- Are we fulfilling our duties of praying, giving, and fasting to connect with God through the Holy Spirit to find answers?

On the flip side, when facing financial hardships or a lack of funds, you may feel God is to blame or God is the last resort. That's when the questioning begins regarding your life's actions. Questions such as…

- God, if you love me, why is this happening now?
- What am I doing wrong?
- Is there no way out for me?

Sometimes, emotions and situations influence the answers to these questions. Understand and acknowledge God is not to blame, nor does He want to be the last resort!

Our Father should be first in all we do, after all, Philippians 4:19 (ERV) reminds us that God uses His glorious riches to give us everything we need through Jesus Christ.

If you are reading this book, it is because you want to unlock financial blessings and enjoy the full life God has promised you. So, prepare for a Financial FAST.

Philippians 4:19 (ERV)
My God will use his glorious riches to give you everything you need.

PRESCRIPTION: Financial FAST

IN THE BEGINNING

The Notice

My husband and I tithed on a regular basis. We gave additional money for outreach programs in our church, along with our time. We volunteered our time in our church as well as other churches along with assisting with a few outreach programs in the community. Not to mention, we both worked, and at one point, attended school. We did all this on top of taking care of a family.

Everything was good, and we balanced life, finances, family, and our commitment to God.

One day, I was interviewing the executive director of a non-profit for an article I was writing for another non-profit blog. During the meeting, I heard a small voice say, "Tell her what kind of job you have." It made no sense to me, but I told her exactly what the voice said. After that, I began to tell her how I worked as a budget analyst and accountant.

She smiled and began to tell me how she had gone through many bookkeepers and accountants who had not maintained or tracked the organization's finances properly. At that point, we both acknowledged that it was God speaking to me.

She offered me a job in her organization as financial officer. I told my husband the story, and we prayed on it. Taking that job would mean many changes for our family. Most of the changes were for the best except the lower pay and no health insurance.

But, how could we consider the changes in finances and health insurance options against a God-given position? With that said, we agreed that I would fill the position.

The transition was smooth; the work was tedious and fulfilling. It consisted of long hours, late nights, and early mornings at work and home, during kids' basketball games, and weekends. I gave my all to getting the organization's financials in order and the bills on a regular pay schedule.

A few months into the job, the primary funding stopped. The organization's funds were frozen. Thankfully, there were other means of income, but it was not enough to sustain the business. I prayed every day, but on this day, I prayed harder than ever. I was more worried about the company being able to pay bills, employees, and taking care of clients more so than myself getting paid because I was holding on to God's promise in Matthew 6:33.

With each day, less funding was received, employees started to resign, office equipment was taken away, and bills began to go to collections. I was not praying anymore; I was now crying to God.

Lord, you brought me here! What am I to do?

At this point, I had been working without pay for months. My household was suffering, bills were piling up, the mortgage was due, our daughter's college fees were due, and we had no means to survive on. This was in addition to us having no tithes to give. So, we started keeping a running total of what we owed God, all the while paying the bills to survive every day.

With each day and week, I began to worry more and more about money. My focused turned away from God and on job searching, worrying about making payments on time, keeping the house, and the stress of the family relationships. In the midst of losing hair, feeling useless, forgotten, and just tired, I began to pray and ask to myself, "Am I really holding onto Matthew 6:33?" I realized that I was not!

Matthew 6:33 (VOICE)
Seek first the kingdom of God and His righteousness, and then all these things will be given to you too.

Financial Revelation

When I realized that I was not holding on to Matthew 6:33, I began to cry. I also started to question myself on how we could possibly owe God. My heart was hurting, and my spirit was shaken.

Our life's balance began to get away from us. We started to face more trials every day in our daily relationships. Trials in our marriage, finances, kids, work, and how we spent our time. I noticed a decline in church attendance from the internal embarrassment of our debt to God and us feeling as though we could not tithe. Work declined for my husband as well and unfortunately, the organization I was working for went out of business.

My heart was crying, and I was on my knees daily praying. I cried out, "God, what now? How are we going to live? How can I manage what we do not have? How can we pay the mortgage and bills? How are we going to eat? How? How? What now? Father help?"

As I was praying, I began to reflect on God's hands on my family to include myself, the blessings He bestowed on us, the enemy He conquered for us, the strongholds He broke for us, and the life He has given us.

I asked myself, "If God has done so much for us, why am I so troubled now?"

Honestly, I was troubled because I was not holding on to His promise. I felt helpless because I did not have a job and my husband had taken on a part-time job. Job searching, along with interviewing, can both be horrible because of the unknowns. Interviewers tend to focus on things like over qualification, not being qualified enough, quality of my resume submission and so on. I questioned whether I said too much or if I'd said too little; the questions were endless.

Again, I was not holding on to God's promise!

I began reading daily devotionals and spending time with God on purpose. 1 Corinthians 15:58 lingered with me. I say lingered because my email signature block included two quotes that are very similar to this scripture. I told myself to get it together and focus on what is important at that moment.

Quote #1: *Daily work takes on eternal significance when it is done for God (author unknown).*

Quote #2: *When you keep your eyes on Christ, everything will come into focus (author unknown).*

I had been ignoring my reminders of God's promises. It was time for me to refocus and get back on track with what God had instructed me to do. I decided to build a more intimate relationship with Him, and He promised to take care of everything else.

I established an action plan!

First, I began to repent and asked for forgiveness for not attending church regularly and for all of my sins. After that, I started reading a daily devotional in the morning and one in the evening. I also began waking up before anyone in my household to pray. On mornings when I did not know what to say, I recited the Lord's Prayer (Matthew 6:9-13), all the while thanking Him for his favor and asking Him to lead my steps each day. Then, I started researching finances in the Bible.

Corinthians 15:58 (MSG)
With all this going for us, my dear, dear friends, stand your ground. And don't hold back. Throw yourselves into the work of the Master, confident that nothing you do for him is a waste of time or effort.

PRESCRIPTION: Financial FAST

The Vision

As I was researching finances in the Bible and understanding prayer, one of the most important connections that can be made with God, I began praying on the scriptures. Not only did I pray about the scriptures I read, I started trying to apply them to my everyday life.

Matthew 6:25-34 (KJV) reads,
"Therefore, I say unto you, take no thought for your life, what ye shall eat, or what ye shall drink; nor yet for your body, what ye shall put on. Is not the life more than meat, and the body than raiment? Behold the fowls of the air: for they sow not, neither do they reap, nor gather into barns; yet your heavenly Father feedeth them. Are ye not much better than they? Which of you by taking thought can add one cubit unto his stature? And why take ye thought for raiment? Consider the lilies of the field, how they grow; they toil not, neither do they spin: And yet I say unto you, that even Solomon in all his glory was not arrayed like one of these. Wherefore, if God so clothe the grass of the field, which today is, and tomorrow is cast into the oven, shall he not much more clothe you, O ye of little faith? Therefore, take no thought, saying, what shall we eat? or, what shall we drink? or, Wherewithal shall we be clothed? (For after all these things do the Gentiles seek:) for your heavenly Father knoweth that ye have need of all these things. But seek ye first the kingdom of God, and his righteousness; and all these things shall be added unto you. Take therefore no thought for the morrow: for the morrow shall take thought for the things of itself. Sufficient unto the day is the evil thereof."

What is your lesson from these scriptures?

_____

_____

_____

How can you apply these scriptures to your everyday life?

_____

_____

_____

According to Matthew, during Jesus' walk on Earth, He understood the burden and destruction that worry brought to His people. We still carry these burdens to this day! He tells us in verse 25, not to worry about the things we need to live, and continues to help us envision how our Father truly loves and will provide for us.

As I repeatedly read those scriptures, I began to cry and ask myself, "Why am I worrying? My Father is clearly taking care of me! That same night, I had a vision and a dream, both of which outlined a book. I was so excited that I woke up out of my sleep and wrote everything down that I could remember. It was so detailed, and I felt blessed that God was delivering a message to me.

The next morning, I started writing, and then it happened. I let life consume me! Placing what God showed me on my TO DO LIST.

Like a child who has knowingly disobeyed her parent, I felt so sorry, sad, and heartbroken.

My Father knew that I was going to let the world and everyday life take my attention from Him. I was on my knees, tearfully asking for forgiveness. If you know my Father like I do, He has forgiven me; He has forgiven us. I learned from this life's lesson to be obedient, forgive myself, and help others know our Father through my testimonies.

I am writing this book to answer prayers because God wants us to know He hears our tearful prayers and pleas. He wants to help us live our lives to the fullest with Him.

Matthew 6:33 (ERV)
What you should want most is God's kingdom and doing what He wants you to do. Then He will give you all these other things you need.

PRESCRIPTION: Financial FAST

Key Point #1 - Scripture

Reading and studying the scriptures is fundamental to helping decipher God's intentions. God planned for His word to be a lifeline for interpreting every situation and a source of direction. Scriptures should also build faith and lead to salvation, while nurturing spiritual maturity.

Moses clearly outlines this in Deuteronomy 8:3 as he is reminding the Israelites to remember God leading them out of Egyptian slavery.

Deuteronomy 8:3 (ERV)
> He humbled you and let you be hungry. Then he fed you with manna—something you did not know about before. It was something your ancestors had never seen. Why did the Lord do this? He did this because he wanted you to know that it is not just bread that keeps people alive. People's lives depend on what the Lord says.

We must do the same! Remember where God led us from and remain humble by being obedient, reading scriptures, and praying for direction. We cannot afford to be prideful and forget what our Father has graciously done in our lives or fail to learn and apply the lessons of the Bible to our lives.

God is alive and real. We cannot live on bread alone; our lives depend on God!

Image this: Jesus arrived in Jordan to be baptized by John the Baptist. John instantly realized that he should not be baptizing Jesus, but Jesus kindly tells him to do what is right. So, John baptized Jesus, and as He was coming up, the heavens opened, and the Spirit of God descended upon him, as the Father affirmed Him, saying, "This is my beloved Son, in whom I am well pleased" (Matthew 3:13-17(ESV)).

Jesus was filled with the Holy Spirit and then led to the wilderness to be tempted by the devil. This was after He'd fasted for 40 days and nights, so he was *hungry*. While being hungry in the wilderness, the devil tempted Jesus. Matthew 4:4(ERV) states Jesus said, *"The Scriptures say, 'It is not just bread that keeps people alive. Their lives depend on what God says"* referencing Deuteronomy 8:3.

This resonates so powerfully with me!

In Matthew 4:4 Jesus references Deuteronomy 8:3 which Moses had spoken to the Israelites in the Old Testament regarding being fed by the Father. After the final temptation Jesus said in Matthew 4:19, *"Get away from me, Satan! The Scriptures say, "You must worship the Lord your God and Serve only him!"*

If Jesus, our example, walked by faith and used scriptures as His strength for His daily walk with God, how are you and I to respond to everyday temptations in our finances and spending?

Write your thoughts?

_____

_____

_____

_____

Describe how Matthew 4:4 and 4:19 can be used in our everyday lives?

_____

_____

_____

_____

_____

Matthew 4:4 (ERV)
Jesus answered him, "The Scriptures say, 'It is not just bread that keeps people alive. Their lives depend on what God says.'"

FINANCIAL FAST

What is a Financial FAST?

Similar to a biblical fast, a financial fast is the voluntary abstinence or evaluation of unnecessary worldly goods/services for a spiritual purpose. Voluntarily abstaining from or evaluating daily expenses will assist in understanding individual management of your God-given resources. These are resources that He provides for His glory and the enhancement of His kingdom.

The Financial FAST will help you understand, build, and strengthen your relationship with God, money, and people. It will also help you to unclutter your soul, be more sensitive to the Holy Spirit and become obedient with your finances. This will also help you to tap into the power of God through praying, giving, and fasting.

Malachi 3:10 is an example of God's promise for wellness through obedience. In this verse, Malachi clearly tells us that God promises blessings if we are obedient and faithful with what we have right now. So, we must decide to honor God with our money. This may be done through donations, contributions, tithes (a tenth of earnings), or however God leads you.

The Bible describes how many tithed with such items as produce, livestock, property, silver, etc., and this is the model we should follow. Not only can we tithe monetarily, but also time through volunteering to help others and the church, providing food to help feed those in need or donating food to shelter and food banks, and property which can be as simple as giving someone a warm place to stay. Tithing and giving can be limitless, depending on one's honest, heartfelt, creative intent.

Take a moment to meditate on those few examples of tithing. List some ways that you currently honor God:

_____

_____

Before going any further, let's have a conversation on strengthening our relationship with our Father through prayer. I told you how putting God first was the start of my action plan and discussed tithing to honor God.

Honestly reflect and write about your prayer life now:

_____

_____

_____

_____

*Your answers will help you later to discern your steps during the Financial FAST.

Communicating or talking to God through prayer, along with reading the Bible and listening to the Holy Spirit are essential to building and strengthening your relationship with our Father.

Take time to meditate on the title father, but do not think about your earthly father. Instead, consider God, the Father.

Reflect on your life and envision times that you have seen His hands touching your life, turning hard situations around for your good and conquering your enemies. Think about the times when He's promoted you, helped you to endure a storm, and the many times He's saved your life. Also consider when you've witnessed Him doing these things in the lives of others.

As you reflect and envision God in your life, in the space below write down your feelings and how that moment changed you:

_____

_____

_____

_____

PRESCRIPTION: Financial FAST

This should encourage you to want a strong, intimate relationship with God. God, the Father, who planned your life before birth, who knows the number of hairs on your head (see Matthew 10:30 ERV), and sent His one and only Son, Jesus, to walk the Earth and set the example for our lives.

A Financial FAST is an opportunity to build a relationship with God. To build a relationship, we must understand what is currently going on in our lives and how it gives an account of our hearts to God. To understand, we must physically assess our relationship with God and money.

As you continue reading through the book, referencing scriptures and answering questions, ask the Holy Spirit for guidance. Ask Him to teach you how to interpret and apply what you are learning so that you can align yourself with God's purpose for your life.

Create an action plan, detailing how you are going to build an intimate relationship with God daily. Make sure to pray for guidance, have a conversation with God!

My Action Plan:

_____

_____

_____

_____

_____

_____

_____

Matthew 10:30 (ERV)
God even know how many hairs are on your head.

Key Point #2 - Obedience

The Bible gives instructions on how to be obedient, specifically with finances. Each verse is plainly written to demonstrate how not to allow money to become an idol. In Luke 3:14, Luke tells us not to extort money and don't falsely accuse people, but be content with your pay. In Ecclesiastes 5:10, Solomon says *"Whoever loves money never has enough; whoever loves wealth is never satisfied with their income."* Again, Solomon warns us in Proverbs 13:11 that dishonest money dwindles away, but whoever gathers money little by little makes it grow.

Read and *meditate* on these verses, and then answer the questions below. (Luke 3:14 (NIV), Ecclesiastes 5:10 (NIV), & Proverbs 13:11 (NIV).

How do you feel about how you earn and spend money?

_____

_____

_____

Does it control you or do you control it?

_____

_____

_____

Not only does the Bible give examples of financial obedience, but it also gives examples of how money can be a blessing. Through stewardship of His resources, God wants to bless us. 1 Timothy 6:17-19 (AMP) explains worldly riches are uncertain, but true certainty is found in trusting God who gives richly and generously. The Bible also reveals in Luke 12:48 (MSG) that *"with great gifts comes great responsibility"* responsibility in honoring God through faithful stewardship, good works, and giving (sharing resources with others). Those following His guidance are laying up for themselves riches that endure forever a good foundation for the future.

PRESCRIPTION: Financial FAST

Even in asking the Holy Spirit for assistance and humbling ourselves, acquiring and/or spending money is an everyday battle that we must all face. Our relationship with God helps us to better understand God's perspective on finances. Our relationship or attitude toward money is based on what we have experienced growing up, what we see every day and what we perceive as right or wrong.

For example, we can evaluate our parents' management of money as we were growing up, it could have been something like this, *"Baby I'm sorry, but we just cannot afford that right now"* or vice versa you may have been able to get everything you want.

Some of us may have worked during our childhood to help support our families, which we only earned money not managed it. At any point on the spectrum, we cannot fully determine how money was handled only the outcome. So, if we want to change the outcome as well as break the generational misunderstanding of money management we must understand our current relationship with God, money, and others then determine our next steps.

Pray aloud:
Thank You, Father, for supplying me with everything I need to enjoy life as you promised. Holy Spirit I ask you to help humble my heart every day to be a good steward of what God has given me, in doing good works and selflessly sharing with others. In Jesus' name, Amen!

Consider the parable of the talents in Matthew 25:14-30, in this parable a man entrusted his servants with his possessions according to their abilities with the result being each servant making a profit equal to what he was given except the servant who was afraid to trust his abilities given by God to generate a profit. There is a lesson we must grasp from the scriptures.

LESSON: Do not let *fear* keep you from experiencing God's financial blessings!

So, what is your lesson from this passage?

_____

_____

_____

What are your abilities or gifts from God? Are you using them accordingly?

_____

_____

_____

_____

Identify any fears that are holding you back from God's blessings.

_____

_____

_____

_____

How can you conquer your fears? Find scripture(s) to support your answer.

_____

_____

_____

_____

How can this lesson be applied to your Financial FAST?

_____

_____

_____

Matthew 25:29 (ERV)
Everyone who uses what they have will get more. They will have much more than they need. But people who do not use what they have will have everything taken away from them.

PRESCRIPTION: Financial FAST

Why do I need a Financial FAST?

As a seasoned or new believer, when studying the Bible, coupled with your personal walk, there are aspects of your current life that must die so your new life in Christ can shine brightly. Meaning, the old habits must be crucified. In crucifying one's self, God will see your efforts along with the desires of your heart. He will also provide endurance and grace through the Holy Spirit. This will help you through the changes during the Financial FAST.

The Financial FAST is needed to ensure that we, as Christians, are good stewards of the gifts that God has graciously entrusted to us! Good stewardship of money is the righteous handling of money. To help visualize the FAST, the table below shows a comparison between a Biblical and Financial FAST.

Biblical FAST	Financial FAST
Refraining from food for a spiritual purpose	Refraining from unnecessary worldly goods/services for a spiritual purpose
Part of a deep, intimate, powerful relationship with God	Part of a deep, intimate, powerful relationship with God
Uncluttered, peaceful spirit, sensitive to God	Uncluttered, peaceful spirit, sensitive to God
Source of Power (Giving, Praying Fasting) – Threefold cord (Ecclesiastes 4:12 ESV)	Source of Power (Giving, Praying, and Fasting) – Threefold cord

The Financial FAST will not only help us to evaluate our current financial situations and remind us of our stewardship, but it will also allow us to dive deeper into a relationship with our Father, seeking His guidance and instruction.

Understanding stewardship will help you better understand a need for a Financial FAST.

Financial Stewardship is utilizing and managing all resources God provides for His glory and the betterment of His creation. In the first letter of Paul to the Corinthians, Paul discussed how God entrusted him with the responsibility of preaching the gospel. Like Paul, we must know and understand our responsibilities. Along with knowing and understanding our responsibilities, we must also be faithful to God, whether we receive rewards of material goods or not. Paul chose to be faithful to God, preach the Gospel and make God's word known. What has God entrusted you to do?

_____

_____

_____

Are you being faithful with what God has entrusted you to do? If so, how? If not, how can you change?

_____

_____

_____

One thing is known ... God has entrusted us with the ability to earn money. With that in mind, we should put Him first in our finances.

How are you putting God first in your finances?

_____

_____

_____

_____

_____

1 Corinthians 9:17-19 (ERV)
For I do this of my own will, I have a reward, but if not of my own will, I am entrusted with a stewardship. What then is my reward? That in my preaching I may present the gospel free of charge, so as not to make full use of my right in the gospel. For though I am free from all, I have made myself a servant to all, that I might win more of them.

PRESCRIPTION: Financial FAST

Key Point #3 - Tithe

Remembering that everything received is a gift from God, we must put Him first in our lives. There is no better way to praise and worship God than through cheerful giving (2 Cor. 9:7) or tithing. **Tithing** is wholeheartedly giving the first 10% of your income to God. Part of thanking and honoring God for what He has done, is doing, and will do in your life is achieved not only through prayer, but also tithing.

Have you ever noticed that part of Worship Service is tithing?

Proverbs 3:9 (AMP)
Honor the Lord with your wealth and with the first fruits of all your crops (income)

2 Corinthians 9:7 (AMP)
Let each one give [thoughtfully and with purpose] just as he has decided in his heart, not grudgingly or under compulsion, for God loves a cheerful giver [and delights in the one whose heart is in his gift].

Malachi 3:8-12 (MSG)
"Begin by being honest. Do honest people rob God? But you rob me day after day. "You ask, 'How have we robbed you?' "The tithe and the offering—that's how! And now you're under a curse—the whole lot of you—because you're robbing me. Bring your full tithe to the Temple treasury, so there will be ample provisions in my Temple. Test me in this and see if I don't open heaven itself to you and pour out blessings beyond your wildest dreams. For my part, I will defend you against marauders, protect your wheat fields and vegetable gardens against plunderers." The Message of God-of-the-Angel-Armies. You'll be voted 'Happiest Nation.' You'll experience what it's like to be a country of grace." God-of-the-Angel-Armies says so.

Read and *meditate* on the above verses.

What does tithing mean to you?

_____

_____

_____

_____

Do you cheerfully give or tithe according to the scripture? Why or Why not?

_____

_____

_____

All blessings, not just financial blessings, are graciously given to us when we honor God.

From our hearts, we must trust and believe in Him as well as align our thoughts and actions with His word and Jesus' examples. It has already been declared, *For I know the plans I have for you," says the LORD. "They are plans for good and not for disaster, to give you a future and a hope (Jeremiah 29:11 AMP). Where your treasure is, there your heart will be also* (Matthew 6:21 AMP).

I understand that sometimes there is only enough money to pay the bills, if that! In this case, we must remember God knows our hearts. If God is first in our lives and we are upholding His love for others and devoting time to Him, along with volunteering at church, we are storing up treasures for ourselves in heaven.

Are you investing your heart in God or money?
(Be honest with yourself!)

_____

_____

_____

This was where my husband and I had to be totally honest and learn to lean on God.

We sat and prayed, thought, and reflected on both God and money. We agreed that we had not been honest with finances. Gratefulness filled our hearts for the gifts God had given to us, but we knew we were taking advantage of the money God blessed us to make with our jobs.

PRESCRIPTION: Financial FAST

Remember, we owed God! We paid bills before tithing. Then we asked God to help us!

We were wrong. This time, we went before God together and asked for forgiveness and guidance going forward. If you are married, it is not all about you, but you and your spouse together as one.

God must come first in the relationship, the household ... everything!

Together, we agreed that ten percent of our income will go to God through tithing. God will receive His just due, even if it meant we'd have to tithe online immediately after getting paid to ensure that we weren't tempted to sporadically spend any money. Tithing online was a way of removing the temptation and being obedient because of our ***LOVE*** for God and what He has done in our lives.

Then, our household changed, and my company went out of business. Money was tight; we paid what we could in tithe, but the difference this time was we both volunteered our services at church and to others in need. So, what we could not pay in tithe, we paid in service to others and the church.

Pray and *ask* yourself, am I robbing God?

After praying, write your first thoughts below and scriptures that resonate with you. Discuss what God is trying to tell you through your thoughts and scripture.

_____

_____

_____

Pray aloud:

God, please forgive me for not being obedient with the blessings you have graciously given me. You provide for my needs each and every day. Holy Spirit guide me in working towards being a good steward of my blessings especially my financial blessings. In Jesus' name, Amen!

How did I get here?

We can think of many reasons that have led us to this point, but the primary reason is the *misunderstanding of God and money.* If you and I were to honestly evaluate our lifestyles, motives, and choices, we would figure out how we got to the point we are at in our lives and finances.

To determine a prescription, a doctor must first understand the illness, right? Similarly, for the Financial FAST to be effective, you must first understand your current money relationship and status!

Action:
- Download, save, or print your current month's bank statement (CSV - Excel spreadsheet)
- Analyze each transaction for that month
- Review and compare withdrawals and deposits

Spending: The payout of money in purchasing goods or services.
Describe your spending: (Is it planned or budgeted spending? Why or Why not?)

_____

_____

_____

_____

Purchases: The action of buying goods or services.
Evaluate your purchases: (Are your purchases planned/budget or necessary? Be sure to include any unnecessary fees/charges)

_____

_____

_____

_____

PRESCRIPTION: Financial FAST

Living within your means: Not spending more than you earn.
Are you living within your means? If no, why not?

_____

_____

_____

Is tithe included in your withdrawals? Why or Why not?

_____

_____

_____

_____

This review of your financial statement is very important in understanding your current financial standing. It should help to enlighten you regarding your personal spending habits.

Detail any changes in spending that you plan to make.

_____

_____

_____

_____

Now that you have reviewed your financial statement in detail, let's try answering the questions from Key Point #2 - Obedience again.

How do you feel about how you spend money?

_____

_____

_____

_____

_____

Does it control you or do you control it? Explain.

_____

_____

_____

_____

_____

_____

Hebrews 13:5-6 (MSG)
Don't be obsessed with getting more material things. Be relaxed with what you have. Since God assured us, "I'll never let you down, never walk off and leave you," we can boldly quote, God is there, ready to help; I'm fearless no matter what. Who or what can get to me?

PRESCRIPTION: Financial FAST

Now, that you have had an opportunity to review your financial statement and re-evaluate your feelings about money and how you spend it, did the answers to these questions change? Honestly detail why or why not.

_____

_____

_____

_____

_____

_____

While meditating on the answers to these questions, let me guide you to more scriptures.

The next few scriptural verses are in Ecclesiastes. As I researched this book to find the author, it is arguably King Solomon, and the book was written sometime between 931 and 935 B.C. (Before Christ). The author and timeframe are important because Solomon references true wisdom in Ecclesiastes! The book discusses how in a confused and fallen world, there is a need to fear God and balance life and work. Is that not what we are facing every day? Though we are incapable of understanding God's ways, we can cling to, trust in, and keep His commandments to help with everyday problems.

When I think about income, the first thought I have is work or a job. Employment, whether you own or work for a business, is our primary means of making money. Whether we like it or not, we have to work to obtain money to live. Do you agree?

_____

_____

_____

Frances Armfield

Read and *meditate* on Ecclesiastes 4: 4-6. Write your first thoughts and the words that resonate with you the most from the scriptures. What do you think God is trying to tell you?

_____

_____

_____

_____

_____

_____

_____

_____

_____

_____

Ecclesiastes 4: 4-6 (ERV)
Then I thought, "Why do people work so hard?" I saw people try to succeed and be better than other people. They do this because they are jealous. They don't want other people to have more than they have. Jealous competition is senseless. It is like trying to catch the wind. Some people say, "It is foolish to fold your hands and do nothing. If you don't work, you will starve to death." Maybe that is true. But I say it is better to be satisfied with the few things you have than always struggling to get more.

PRESCRIPTION: Financial FAST

In my household, money earned from employment is not only used to pay bills, but also to buy the latest Apple gadget for my husband, the latest video game for my youngest child, trending clothes for my daughter and I, helping others, tithes, and the list goes on. Are all these items needed to live every day? I am the first to say *NO*, my husband and I tried to give our kids what we did not have growing up and spare disappointment to a degree in their lives. We were setting them up for future disappointments and reinforcing the worldly view of needs. After studying, Ecclesiastes 4:4-6 (ERV), which clearly tells us *to be satisfied with the few things we have instead of struggling to get more*, we had to repent and ask for forgiveness.

Our gracious Father's love forgave us, but we had to take action moving forward. Before any purchases, we would come together, pray, and ask God to show us direction. In doing that, God revealed another aspect of our lives that we were not putting Him first. So, for us, this was another lesson; we learned to put God first in every situation, not just a few or particular situations, but *ALL* situations.

Talk about a humbling situation, this was one of them!

We had to change our perspectives because we live in a world that continually introduces new and upgraded products and services at the blink of an eye. We, meaning the world, have proven that we cannot live without having something new or improved, convenient, and at any cost! But, it is up to us as families and individuals to turn this around and praise God, thanking Him for His favor in our finances through tithing, fasting, and helping others.

Why do you work?

_____

_____

_____

_____

_____

Honestly assess your current spending habits and the reason you work. Review your answers to the questions in the text I've asked all the way up to this point. How do you think you got to this point in your life, finances, and job?

_____

_____

_____

_____

_____

_____

_____

_____

_____

Pray aloud:
Holy Spirit, I am asking your help to encourage me to trust God in my everyday confusing world. Teach me to fear Him and keep His commandments, even though I cannot understand everything going on around me. Help me meditate on and recite the scriptures I treasure in my heart so that I can walk in peace with confidence every day, knowing my Father is with me during each step, decision, thought, and action. In Jesus' name, Amen!

PRESCRIPTION: Financial FAST

LEAP OF FAITH

Necessity or Nicety?

Before moving into the meat of the message, an important aspect of the Financial FAST, we must distinguish the difference between a **necessity and a nicety**. This is the difference between a need for daily living and something nice that we think we need for daily living.

*The niceties are the items that we need to abstain from or remove during our Financial FAST.

Let's determine what is necessary for everyday life. God's priority for our lives is ensuring our wellness from the inside out. He patiently provides for our needs and wants to make sure our souls are flourishing and healthy.

For the soul to be healthy and flourish, we know the basic needs are food, clothing and shelter. So, a basic budget should include an allotted amount for grocery, rent or mortgage (unless you own your home), and clothing and/or maintenance of.

Elaborating on those few items ...

1. Some grocery stores are now Superstores, so shopping requires great discipline. They have everything you want, need, and did not think about. I find it helpful to maintain a simple list of items that *need to be replenished* around the house.
2. Rent or Mortgage payments usually are due on the first of the month. I find it helpful, if needed, to divide and conquer. Depending on when you receive your income, split the amount between pay periods. For example, if you happen to get paid on the 1st and 15th of each month, split the payment between the 15th of the previous month and the first of the current month. Review it on paper, comparing it to a calendar, noting when you receive your income to make sure it works for you. Also consider if this arrangement will allow your payment to be made on time.

3. Clothing and clothing maintenance: This is another area that needs discipline. For children, we know they grow fast, and it is easier to determine when their wardrobe needs to be replenished. As for the adults, it's not so easy! When establishing a budget amount for this particular line item, think about *necessity*. Ask yourself, do I really need:
   - To take my clothing to the dry cleaners or can I refresh and iron them myself?
   - A new outfit or shoes because they are on sale?

These are just some basic suggestions to help guide your thoughts and understanding of necessities versus niceties so that you can seek God and ask Him how you should spend and distribute your funds.

The first step to creating a budget is praying for God's guidance. After all, He has blessed you with a resource to make money. We must seek and confide in Him every step of the way to ensure we are strengthening our relationships with Him.

Write your own prayer below, asking God to help you establish a closer, stronger relationship with Him. Do this while learning to use scriptures (His Word) to create a budget and work through the Financial FAST.

_____

_____

_____

_____

_____

_____

3 John 1:2 (ESV)
Beloved, I pray that all may go well with you and that you may be in good health, as it goes well with your soul.

PRESCRIPTION: Financial FAST

In Philippians, Apostle Paul learned, and taught satisfaction is not doing, having, or living the way you want, but standing firm, rejoicing in the Lord who knows and faithfully provides your every need.

What are your daily needs?

_____

_____

_____

How are they being supplied? What has the Lord provided?

_____

_____

_____

Are your needs included in your budget? Why or Why not?

_____

_____

_____

_____

_____

Philippians 4:11-13 (ERV)
I am telling you this, but not because I need something. I have learned to be satisfied with what I have and with whatever happens. I know how to live when I am poor and when I have plenty. I have learned the secret of how to live through any kind of situation—when I have enough to eat or when I am hungry, when I have everything I need or when I have nothing. Christ is the one who gives me the strength I need to do whatever I must do.

God equips you and I with strength and whatever else we need to accomplish what He calls us to do. Knowing He faithfully provides and equips us is a remainder to remain positive during any difficulties we may face in everyday life. Right now, working through to financial wellness may be a difficulty for you, but rest assured the Lord is with you.

During this journey, you have begun finding fulfillment through scripture and applying it to your life. As you continue, you will build and strengthen your relationship with the Lord, your Father, through meditation and reflection on verses and how He has loved you throughout your life.

Our Father has called each of us to advance the Gospel. He started developing, perfecting, and bringing to full completion a good work in us and He will finish it (Philippians 1:6 NIV).

Remember, though God is working on us, we must also do our part! We must continue to trust and believe in Him. Not only should we continue to trust and believe in Him, but also cooperate with the counsel of the Holy Spirit in our lives, which Jesus so graciously gave His life for us to possess.

I understand it may be uncomfortable going through your finances now, but the result will be you and God walking hand-in-hand daily. You are allowing God to do work in you as well as your finances, and God to empower your life through your finances.

Don't give up, stay strong, and rely on God! The Apostle Paul also believed that suffering is beneficial. He said in *Romans 5:3-5 (NLT)*…

> *"Because of our faith, Christ has brought us into this place of undeserved privilege where we now stand, and we confidently and joyfully look forward to sharing God's glory. We can rejoice, too, when we run into problems and trials, for we know that they help us develop endurance. And endurance develops strength of character, and character strengthens our confident hope of salvation. And this hope will not lead to disappointment. For we know how dearly God loves us, because he has given us the Holy Spirit to fill our hearts with his love."*

Thanks be to God!

Back to the Basics - FASTing

We have all prayed for God to help resolve our financial situations, but have we experienced His solution? If not, bold prayers and Financial FASTing are ways of engaging our faith until God's promises are fulfilled in our lives. It is being responsible! Responsible for the management of the blessings we have right in front of us.

The tables in this section are basic examples only; please use the spreadsheet in the back of the book to annotate your information.

In the section, **How did I get here?**, we downloaded and reviewed a current bank statement. In reviewing the bank statement, there were exercises to describe your spending as well as evaluate your purchases; this is where that information is useful. This is where we start the Financial FASTing!

Step 1: Calculate your total Income

Income is money you receive on a daily, weekly, or monthly basis. This can be a regular paycheck, assistance, or support type payment. Total income would be the amount paid after taxes or net income (take home amount).

From experience, I suggest using only actual income amounts to establish your budget because projected or anticipated income are not guaranteed. If necessary, add projected or anticipated income once received. There is no worse feeling than establishing a budget based on anticipated funds and finding that you will not receive them, now changes are needed to the budget and payments have to be rearranged to ensure necessary payments are made on time.

Outline your income below:

_____

_____

_____

Step 1	Calculate Income
Work	$
Assistance	$
Support	$
Total Income Amount (add above amounts)	$

The total income amount calculated above will be the basis for all the other parts of your budget. You want to ensure that your expenses *do not* exceed this amount. That is, *live within your means*, which is your total income.

Step 2: Calculate your expenses

Before outlining expenses, let's discuss our basic physical needs. Many different factors in our lives play a part in determining our individual basic physical needs. As part of the Financial FAST, we must humble ourselves, meditate on Philippians 4:11-13, and review the sections **Necessity or Nicety**.
*The niceties are the items that we need to abstain from or remove during our Financial FAST.

What are your basic physical needs?

_____

_____

_____

_____

_____

Pray aloud:
God, give me discipline, wisdom, and understanding about my current financial situation. Reveal to me any unhealthy habits you need me to overcome during this Financial FAST. While learning stewardship in my finances, help me to use this same stewardship in other aspects of my life to increase my faith and encourage others. In Jesus' name, Amen!

PRESCRIPTION: Financial FAST

Now, review your bank statement and compare it with your basic physical needs listing.

- Are there some identified needs that are really wants?
  Wants, for now, are categorized as niceties and should be removed during the FAST.

  _____

  _____

- If so, can they be eliminated from your list?

  _____

  _____

- Are the remaining listed needs your actual needs/expenses for everyday living?

  _____

  _____

- Remember, we must pay what we owe! This includes credit or store cards, loan payments, and any known debts. List them below.

  _____

  _____

  _____

  * *If possible, list these items as expenses, remembering to stay within your means. That may mean only paying the minimum payment for now, as well as abstaining from any further use of the line of credit.*

On the table below, I have added a few items just for thought. Please updated it with your list of expenses and expand as needed, making sure that it corresponds with the timeframe in which you are paid (daily, weekly, bi-weekly, or monthly basis). This should coordinate with the figures calculated in the income section.

For example, if you calculated your income on a bi-weekly basis and your expenses are paid on a monthly basis, ensure you calculate your income for the month (4 weeks) before deducting your expenses. Another option is arranging your expenses to be paid according to your pay period.

Step 2	Expenses
Tithe	$
Shelter (Mortgage/Rent/Utilities)	$
Food	$
Transportation	$
Debt	$
Insurance	$
Other	$
Savings	$
Total Expenses Amount (add above amounts)	$

Step 3: Calculate your budget balance

The budget balance is the residual balance after all expenses are paid. It is the total income minus the total expenses. It should help you to see and understand how God is fulfilling your needs daily.

Step 3	Amount
Total Income	$
Total Expenses	- $
Budget Balance (Remaining Balance)	$

*Evaluate your budget balance.

PRESCRIPTION: Financial FAST

Is your budget balance positive or negative? Explain.

_____

_____

_____

If your budget balance is negative, before making any major adjustments, pray for God's guidance. Knowing God will supply your every need, ask for help deciding what changes can be made to your expenses, so you can live within your income amount or ask God if there are additional financial blessings coming to balance your budget.

Also, ask yourself the following questions:

- Am I being honest with myself about my needs? Explain why or why not.

The niceties or wants are the items that we need to abstain from or remove during our FAST.

_____

_____

_____

- Are there any changes to my expenses that I can afford to make?

_____

_____

_____

_____

Suggestions:

- Plan and cook meals at home, instead of eating out.
- Change cable to online/stream subscription.
- Consider searching for cell phone plans within your budget.
- Sell unused clothes, shoes, books, etc. that are in good condition for consignment or online for extra cash.
- Consider a roommate or renting a room.

Pray for guidance on changes you need to implement in your expenses. Use the lines below to list those changes that are revealed during your prayer time and how you will progressively implement them.

_____

_____

_____

_____

_____

_____

_____

_____

_____

_____

Proverbs 19:1 (ERV)
It is better to be poor and honest than to be a liar and a fool.

PRESCRIPTION: Financial FAST

If your budget balance is positive, pray for God to reveal His next step in your finances. This would also be a good opportunity to consider establishing or continue putting money into savings or investing. Be careful, make sure to ask for God's guidance and do your research on how to save and invest your money wisely!

Mediate and take notes on the following questions:

- Are all your needs met?

_____

_____

_____

_____

- Do you have any outstanding debts that need to be paid?

_____

_____

_____

_____

- Do you owe someone money that you borrowed?

_____

_____

_____

_____

- Is there anyone or any organization that God has asked you to assist financially? According to your budget balance, can you assist as God has asked you? Do you think you would have realized this without working through the Financial FAST? Explain.

_____

_____

_____

_____

_____

_____

_____

_____

_____

_____

_____

Ecclesiastes 7:12 (NLT)
Wisdom and money can get you almost anything, but only wisdom can save your life.

PRESCRIPTION: Financial FAST

I created a sample budget to be used as a guide. As you can see, the income, expenses, and budget balance have been computed based on the calculations outlined in this section.

Financial FASTing Budget (example)

INCOME	Work (2,050 bi-wkly)	$4,100	Tithe (total income*10%)	$435
	Assistance	$0		
	Support	$0		
	Extra Income (recvd Uber)	$250		
	Total Income	$4,350		
EXPENSES	Tithe	$435		
	Shelter (Mortgage/Rent)	$1,780		
	Food	$445		
	Transportation	$490		
	Insurance	$420		
	Debt	$210		
	Other	$295		
	Total Expenses	$4,075		
BUDGET BALANCE	Income	$4,350		
*(income - expenses)	Expense	($4,075)		
	Ending Balance	$275		

Shelter (mthly)	Cost	Food	Cost	Transportation	Cost
Mortgage or rent	$1,400	Grocery (mthly)	$250	Vehicle payment (mthly)	$250
Cable/Internet/Phone Pkg	$125	Dining Out (occasional)	$75	Uber/Lyft/Bus fare	$0
Electricity & Gas	$180	Lunch @ work (mthly)	$120	Insurance (mthly)	$120
Water & sewer	$40			Registration (annual)	$0
Garbage	$35			Fuel (add wkly = mthly)	$120
Maintenance/repairs	$0			Maintenance	$0
Total Shelter	**$1,780**	**Total Food**	**$445**	**Total Transportation**	**$490**

Insurance (mthly)	Cost	Debts (mthly)	Cost	Other	Cost
Home	$250	Credit Card	$65	Entertainment	$25
Vehicle	$120	Store Card	$25	Gym membership	$20
Life	$50	Loan	$120	Clothing	$250
Medical (deducted from pay)	$0				
Total Insurance	**$420**	**Total Debts**	**$210**	**Total Other**	**$295**

A blank copy of this budget is in the back of the book for your use. This exercise is key to helping you see your financial blessings and how you are distributing them. Prayerfully, it has helped you ...

- gain a closer, stronger relationship with God.
- learn to seek Him first in all situations.
- trust that He has your best interest in mind.
- gain confidence in yourself and your finances by putting God first.

After all, He did create you!

Now that we have established the foundation of the Financial FAST with scriptures and built a budget that reveals how we use the blessings of our finances, there are a few more commissions we must embrace. These commissions should be continuous actions that inspire us to persist in our relationship with God to ensure that we'll have treasures in heaven.

Mark 10:22 (AMP)
"You lack one thing: go and sell all your property and give [the money] to the poor, and you will have [abundant] treasure in heaven; and come, follow Me [becoming My disciple, believing and trusting in Me and walking the same path of life that I walk]."

Continuous Actions

Let me clarify, I am not telling you to sell everything you have and give to the poor. I am trying to help you understand your financial blessings so when you are led by the Holy Spirit, you know exactly what you must give because He already knows! It is simply recognizing what we have right now.

Believers have been commissioned to help others learn about, believe in, and obey Jesus (Matthew 28:19 (AMP)). To lead others to Jesus, we have to recognize the blessings at hand and also have faith and patience.

And remember God is able to do the impossible!

In Matthew 17:20, Jesus emphasized to the disciples the importance of the combination of individual faith and the power of God, which produces amazing results, but the key is the request must be in God's will.

Meditate on Matthew 17:20 (AMP).
> He answered, "Because of your little faith [your lack of trust and confidence in the power of God]; for I assure you and most solemnly say to you, if you have [living] faith the size of a mustard seed, you will say to this mountain, 'Move from here to there,' and [if it is God's will] it will move; and nothing will be impossible for you.

Describe your faith:

_____

_____

Would a non-believer be inspired to explore God or the Bible from your faith? Explain.

_____

_____

PRESCRIPTION: Financial FAST

Together, we have uncovered that God created us for a purpose (His will for us) and commissioned us to help others come to Him (The Great Commission). The tools we have discovered to this point empower us to visualize and understand the blessings bestowed on us, building our faith and trust in God. Faith and trust in God are not only tools we must embrace and practice, but the start of helping a non-believer get to know God by having the patience to discuss what we have personally uncovered on our Financial FAST.

Have you ever heard the phrase, "Patience is a virtue"? The proof is in Romans 5:3-4 (ERV); it states, *"Troubles makes us more patient and this patience is proof we are strong, and this proof gives us hope!"* Having patience to have a conversation about experiences, whether good or bad, easy or hard, is what we are commissioned to do. Jesus is living proof that life is not easy, so why would we make our lives look easy, organized, and perfect, when they are not? As former non-believers, we know and understand that it is hard to make the first step to come to Christ, but with patience, understanding, love, and our being able to relate to others, we can help bring many to Christ.

I pray and hope this book has helped you find everyday patience, strengthened your faith and relationship with God, and transformed your thoughts and actions towards managing your finances.

Use it as often as necessary to continuously encourage yourself, or pass it on as a testimony for someone else. I am confident God will do amazing things in your life and the person you pass this book on to. I am confident that He will take you places that only He can because you are working towards aligning yourself with God's plan through prayer, studying the Word, fasting, giving, and personal testimonies.

Romans 5:3-5 (ERV)
And we are also happy with the troubles we have. Why are we happy with troubles? Because we know that these troubles make us more patient. And this patience is proof that we are strong. And this proof gives us hope. And this hope will never disappoint us. We know this because God has poured out his love to fill our hearts through the Holy Spirit he gave us.

REFLECTIONS

Breaking the FAST

Ending or breaking a fast is the most critical step of a biblical fast. It involves reestablishing the foundation of eating, all the while embracing the mental and physical changes that took place during the fasting process. This step involves knowing and understanding the changes of your mind and body. The changes experienced are imperative to continuing your relationship with God through what you have learned during the fast.

I would like to challenge you to do the same with ending the Financial FAST. God's goal through me was to reveal His perspective on life and finances with the emphasis on conditioning the heart from His works in me. Conditioning our hearts will reveal His perspective, but we must first honestly evaluate the current condition of our hearts.

Life and every day experiences contribute to the condition of our hearts and affects our finances. My personal experiences involved aspects of life that we all share. Sharing my experiences and how my family and I worked through those hardships is my personal testimony for you. I am not perfect, and I do not profess to be Godlike, but my heart is the key that allows the Holy Spirit to guide and use my life as a living example for others.

As you journeyed through each page of this book, the Holy Spirit worked to answer your questions and reveal scriptures that will hopefully ignite your confidence in the Holy Spirit and trust in God. Your confidence and trust will help you recognize the spiritual and financial changes that are needed in your life. Self-discovery and the need for God are important in every aspect of our daily walk in Christ. We must be spiritually and financially responsible for our lives and families. The Financial FAST helped connect the two with scriptures and prayers.

Embrace your journey to a renewed spiritual and financial insight supported by God. Your journey will continue to include struggles, strengths, realizations, perseverance, disappointments, forgiveness, weakness, support, and the list will go on and on, but the difference now

PRESCRIPTION: Financial FAST

is the key. The key is the condition of your HEART, a heart continuously seeking God and expressing His love to others.

I pray this FINACIAL FAST has helped you better understand your purpose in life, starting with a pure heart!

1 Timothy 1:5 (ERV)
The aim of our charge is love that issues from a pure heart and a good conscience and a sincere faith.

Financial FASTing Calculation Tables

Step 1: Calculate total Income	Income
Work	$
Assistance	$
Support	$
Total Income Amount (add above amounts)	$

Step 2: Calculate total expenses	Expenses
Tithe	$
Shelter (Mortgage/Rent)	$
Food	$
Transportation	$
Debt	$
Insurance	$
Other	$
Savings	$
Total Expenses Amount (add above amounts)	$

Step 3: Calculate Budget Balance	Amount
Total Income	$
Total Expenses (subtract from income)	- $
Budget Balance (Remaining Balance)	$

*Personalize section labels to fit your income and expenses.

PRESCRIPTION: Financial FAST

Financial FASTing Budget Worksheet

INCOME					
	Work	$		Tithe (total income*10%) (Total Income x .10)	$
	Assistance	$			
	Support	$		Savings (total income^__% or $ ___) * Decide on a percentage of income or a set amount to put into Savings	$
	Extra Income	$			
	Total Income	$			

EXPENSES		
	Tithe	$
	Shelter/Related Expenses (Mortgage/Rent/Utilities)	$
	Food/Entertainment	$
	Transportation Expenses (Lease/gas/maintenance/repair)	$
	Insurance (Auto/Home/Rental)	$
	Debts	$
	Other	$
	Savings	$
		$
		$
	Total Expenses	$

BUDGET BALANCE		
	Income	$
	Expense (subtract from total expenses)	$
	Ending Balance *(income - expenses)	$

Shelter/Related Expenses	Cost	Food/Entertainment	Cost	Transportation Expenses	Cost
	$		$		$
	$		$		$
	$		$		$
	$		$		$
	$		$		$
	$		$		$
	$		$		$
	$		$		$
Total Shelter	$	Total Food	$	Total Transportation	$

Insurance	Cost	Debts	Cost	Other Expenses	Cost
	$		$		$
	$		$		$
	$		$		$
	$		$		$
	$		$		$
	$		$		$
Total Insurance	$	Total Debts	$	Total Other	$

Frances Armfield

Has the financial FAST helped you to improve your relationship with God and money? If so, how can you share your testimony with others?

_____
_____
_____
_____
_____
_____
_____
_____
_____
_____
_____
_____

Now, that you have an idea on what and how you would share your testimony with others, start sharing!

PRESCRIPTION: Financial FAST

Financial FAST
ACTION PLAN NOTES

Frances Armfield
Financial FAST
ACTION PLAN NOTES

Financial FAST

SCRIPTURES

Bible verse: _____

_____

_____

Bible verse: _____

_____

_____

Bible verse: _____

_____

_____

Bible verse: _____

_____

_____

Bible verse: _____

_____

_____

Frances Armfield
Financial FAST
SCRIPTURES

Bible verse: _____

_____

_____

Bible verse: _____

_____

_____

Bible verse: _____

_____

_____

Bible verse: _____

_____

_____

Bible verse: _____

_____

_____

PRESCRIPTION: Financial FAST

Financial FAST

PRAYERS

Prayer: _____
_____
_____

Prayer: _____
_____
_____

Prayer: _____
_____
_____

Prayer: _____
_____
_____

Prayer: _____
_____
_____

Frances Armfield
Financial FAST
PRAYERS

Prayer: _____

_____

_____

Prayer: _____

_____

_____

Prayer: _____

_____

_____

Prayer: _____

_____

_____

Prayer: _____

_____

_____

www.ingramcontent.com/pod-product-compliance
Lightning Source LLC
Chambersburg PA
CBHW052105110526
44591CB00013B/2356